>YOU+DO-THE÷MATHS

Practise your maths and train with the best.

FLY A
JET FIGHTER

HILARY KOLL AND **STEVE MILLS**

ILLUSTRATED BY **VLADIMIR ALEKSIC**

Created for QED Publishing, Inc. by Tall Tree Ltd
Editor: Jon Richards
Designers: Ed Simkins and Jonathan Vipond

QED Editorial Director: Victoria Garrard
QED Art Director: Laura Roberts-Jensen
QED Editor: Tasha Percy
QED Designer: Krina Patel

First published in the UK in 2014 by
QED Publishing
A Quarto Group company
The Old Brewery, 6 Blundell Street
London, N7 9BH

www.qed-publishing.co.uk

A catalogue record for this book is
available from the British Library.

ISBN 978 1 78171 694 6

Printed in China

CONTENTS

Hi, my name is Katie and I'm a pilot. I'm here to show you how maths can help you fly a jet fighter.

Words in **bold** are explained in the glossary on page 32.

HIGH SPEEDS

Jet fighters are fast, small and very manoeuvrable. They are used in many different roles, including air-to-air combat.

You have been given command of a squadron of jet fighters and their pilots.

Jet fighters are powered by jet engines. These work by air being sucked into the engine, compressed (squashed into a smaller volume), mixed with fuel and then burnt.

Blast of hot gases

Air sucked in

Burning fuel creates a powerful blast of hot gases, which rush out of the back of the engine, pushing the aircraft forwards.

Most jet fighters go faster than the speed of sound – which is about 1200 kilometres per hour (km/h) at sea level. Speeds faster than sound are known as supersonic speeds.

The speed of sound gets slower as the jet fighters climb higher up into the atmosphere.

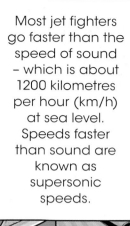

1 How much faster than the speed of sound is a jet fighter going when it is at:

a) 1350 km/h? b) 1420 km/h?
c) 1570 km/h? d) 1650km/h?
e) 1730 km/h? f) 1860 km/h?

2 If a jet fighter is flying at the speed of sound this is known as Mach 1 (pronounced 'Mack one'). If it is flying twice the speed of sound, this is known as Mach 2. What speed is Mach 2?

3 Cars often travel at 80 km/h. How many times faster than 80 km/h is:
a) Mach 1?
b) Mach 2?

4 Work out these speeds:

a) Mach 1·1 is 120 km/h faster than Mach 1. What speed is Mach 1·1?
b) Mach 1·2 is 240 km/h faster than Mach 1. What speed is Mach 1·2?
c) Mach 1·9 is 120 km/h slower than Mach 2. What speed is Mach 1·9?
d) Mach 1·5 is halfway between Mach 1 and Mach 2. What speed is Mach 1·5?

WHAT ABOUT THIS?
Find out the speeds of some other vehicles and see how they compare to a supersonic jet fighter.

DIFFERENT TYPES OF JET FIGHTER

The jet fighter you will fly is called the F-22 Raptor.
The letter 'F' in its name stands for 'fighter'.

During your flight missions, you might come up against fighters from other air forces. Look at the data in this table to compare some of these jet fighters to your own.

JET FIGHTER TYPES

	F-22 RAPTOR	EUROFIGHTER TYPHOON	F-35 LIGHTNING II	CHENGDU J-10
Crew	1	1	1	1
Length	18.9 m	15.96 m	15.67 m	15.49 m
Wingspan	13.56 m	10.95 m	10.7 m	9.75 m
Height	5.08 m	5.28 m	4.33 m	5.43 m
Wing **area**	78.04 m²	51.2 m²	42.7 m²	33.1 m²
Max. takeoff weight	38,000 kg	23,500 kg	31,800 kg	19,277 kg
Max. speed at high altitude	Mach 2.25	Mach 2	Mach 1.6	Mach 2.2

THE HISTORY OF JET FIGHTERS

Part of your training involves learning about the history of jet fighters and their use in combat.

This **timeline** shows some of the key events in the history of jet fighters.

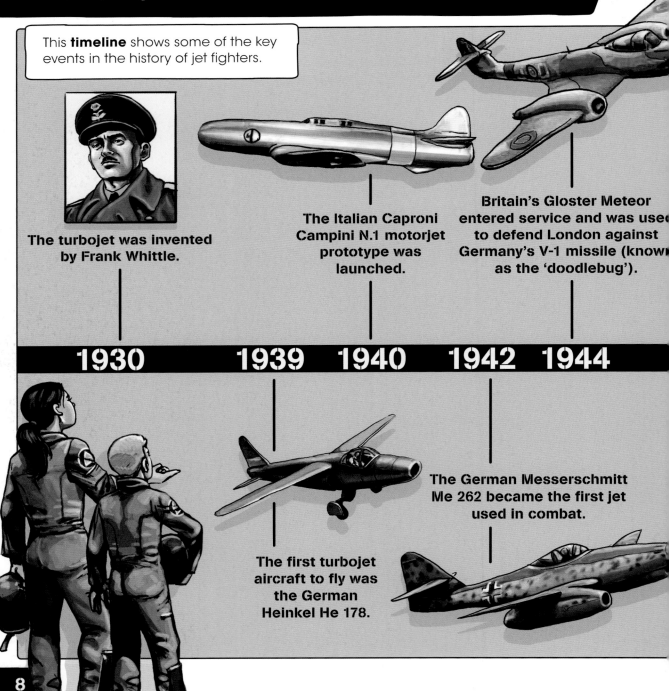

The turbojet was invented by Frank Whittle.

The Italian Caproni Campini N.1 motorjet prototype was launched.

Britain's Gloster Meteor entered service and was used to defend London against Germany's V-1 missile (known as the 'doodlebug').

1930   1939   1940   1942   1944

The first turbojet aircraft to fly was the German Heinkel He 178.

The German Messerschmitt Me 262 became the first jet used in combat.

1. What happened 24 years before the year 1954?

2. Which fighter entered service 16 years after 1939?

3. How many years after the first flight of the Heinkel He 178 did the MiG-19 enter service?

4. How many years after the first turbojet aircraft were launched did the Eurofighter Typhoon enter service?

5. Which fighter entered service 51 years after the Hawker Hunter?

6. How long before the maiden flight of the Chengdu J-20 did the Gloster Meteor enter service?

The Chinese Chengdu J-20 made its first flight.

The British single-seat jet fighter, the Hawker Hunter, entered service.

The Eurofighter Typhoon entered service.

| 1950 | 1954 | 1955 | 2003 | 2005 | 2011 |

The first jet-to-jet dogfight in history occurred over Korea.

The F-22 Raptor entered service.

The Russian MiG-19 entered service.

WHAT ABOUT THIS?
Choose four events from the timeline and work out how many years ago they happened.

JET FIGHTER USES

Every mission you fly will be different! One day you could be involved in air-to-air combat and the next you could be carrying out a vital role escorting other aircraft.

Depending on the mission, a jet fighter could be used for tasks such as reconnaissance (finding out what the enemy is doing)…

…attacking targets on the ground…

…air support for ground troops…

…or escorting other aircraft.

This pie chart shows the proportion of hours that one jet fighter spends doing different operations.

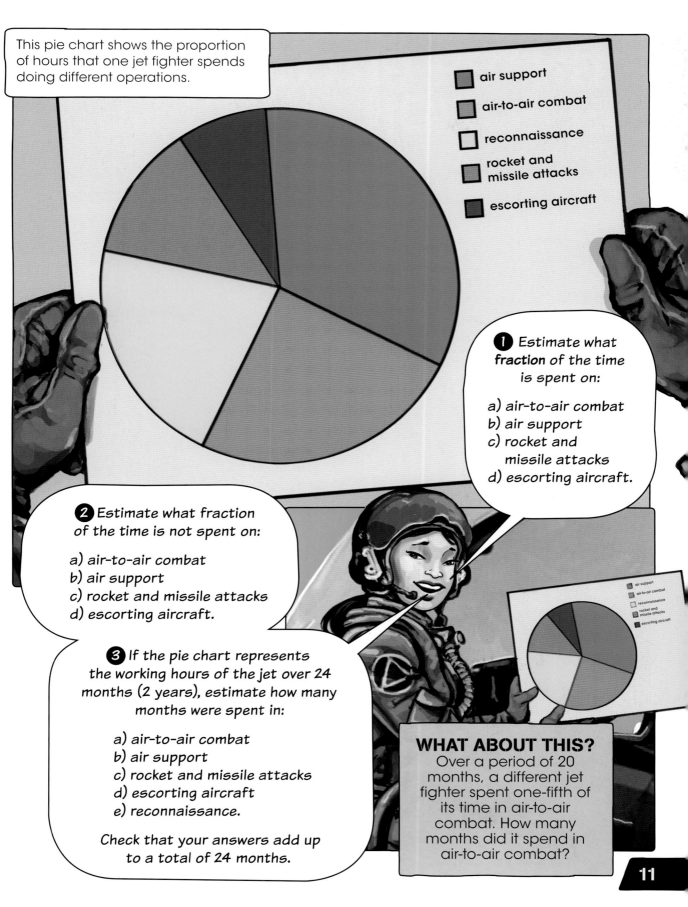

- air support
- air-to-air combat
- reconnaissance
- rocket and missile attacks
- escorting aircraft

1 Estimate what **fraction** of the time is spent on:

a) air-to-air combat
b) air support
c) rocket and missile attacks
d) escorting aircraft.

2 Estimate what fraction of the time is not spent on:

a) air-to-air combat
b) air support
c) rocket and missile attacks
d) escorting aircraft.

3 If the pie chart represents the working hours of the jet over 24 months (2 years), estimate how many months were spent in:

a) air-to-air combat
b) air support
c) rocket and missile attacks
d) escorting aircraft
e) reconnaissance.

Check that your answers add up to a total of 24 months.

WHAT ABOUT THIS?
Over a period of 20 months, a different jet fighter spent one-fifth of its time in air-to-air combat. How many months did it spend in air-to-air combat?

FIGHTER PILOT SELECTION PROCESS

Now you've learnt the basics about your aircraft, it's time to choose the other pilots who will make up your squadron.

Becoming a fighter pilot is extremely difficult as there are not many places available and a lot of people apply.

Applicants must be between 17.5 and 25 years old and be between 168 cm and 188 cm tall.

Fighter pilots must be good problem-solvers and must be confident and calm.

Perfect eyesight is essential for fighter pilots.

The table below shows nine people who would like to apply for the pilot selection process.

1 How many of the candidates are within the correct age range to become a fighter pilot?

2 Which of the candidates are the correct height to become a fighter pilot?

FIGHTER PILOT CANDIDATES

NAME	M/F	AGE	HEIGHT	EYESIGHT
Luke Sharp	Male	19	157.9 cm	perfect
Ben Sherman	Male	16	166.3 cm	not perfect
Theo Wood	Male	24	177.4 cm	perfect
Emily Connor	Female	25	174.3 cm	perfect
Poppy Papadopoulou	Female	28	192.4 cm	perfect
Deepa Gorasia	Female	20	178.2 cm	not perfect
Simon Davis	Male	36	183.1 cm	perfect
Julia Hoffmann	Female	29	184.2 cm	perfect
Devon Richardson	Male	22	169.1 cm	perfect

3 Three of the candidates have the correct height, the preferred age and perfect eyesight. Who are they and are they male or female?

WHAT ABOUT THIS?
Find out your own height and see how many more centimetres you need to grow to be able to apply to be a fighter pilot. How much older do you need to be?

FIGHTER PILOT TRAINING

With your squadron selected, it's time to climb into the cockpit and start your training.

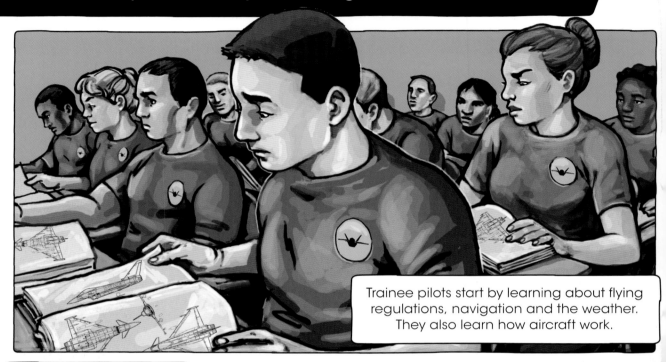

Trainee pilots start by learning about flying regulations, navigation and the weather. They also learn how aircraft work.

They will learn how to fly on flight simulators and training aircraft, before moving onto jet fighters.

The training is very tiring with 12-hour days. This is to ensure that pilots learn to cope with stressful situations.

1 Write the time (using the words 'o'clock', 'past' or 'to') that a pilot starts:

a) Physical training
b) Emergency procedures test
c) Flight schedule planning
d) Flight grading
e) Daily written exam.

2 Write how many minutes there are from the start of each activity below, to the start of the activity the pilot must do next:

a) Morning briefing
b) Flight schedule planning
c) Flight grading
d) Daily written exam.

A TYPICAL DAY IN PILOT TRAINING

06:00	Studying flight regulations
07:00	Physical training
09:00	Morning briefing
09:30	Emergency procedures test
10:15	Studying weather conditions
10:45	Flight schedule planning
12:00	Meal time
12:30	Simulated flight practice
15:55	Flight grading
16:40	Daily written exam
18:00	Rest and private study time

3 Write the activity that the pilot is doing at:

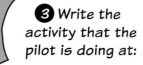

a)

b)

c)

d)

e)

f)

WHAT ABOUT THIS?

If a pilot trains for 12 hours each day, six days a week and for eight weeks, how many hours of training is this?

PILOT CALCULATIONS

While on a mission, you will have to make very quick calculations about a wide range of things.

These will include calculating the distance to other aircraft, including your target.

The information from your fighter's displays will also help you to work out how much fuel you have left and whether you need to **ascend** or **descend**.

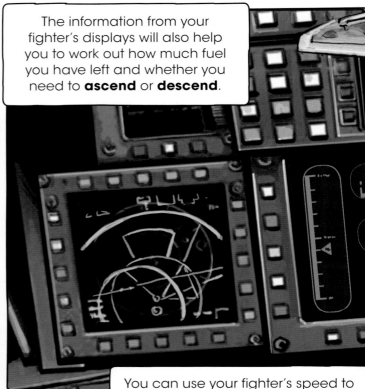

You can use your fighter's speed to work out how long it will take to reach a target.

ROAR

You are flying at 9.4 km above the ground, going at a speed of 510 km/h.

The controller tells you to descend to 5.5 km above the ground. You have also been advised to slow down to 360 km/h.

① How many kilometres must you descend?

② By how many kilometres per hour must you slow down?

③ Once you reach 360 km/h, you stay at this speed. How long would it take you to travel:

   a) 360 km? b) 180 km? c) 90 km?

④ If you are flying at 360 km/h, how far would you travel in:

   a) one minute?
   b) two minutes?
   c) three minutes?
   d) five minutes?

⑤ a) How long would a 50-km journey take flying at 500 km/h?
   b) How much longer would it take flying at 200 km/h?

⑥ How much longer would a 90-km journey take flying at 540 km/h than at 900 km/h?

WHAT ABOUT THIS?
If you know that your jet fighter is travelling at a speed of 12 kilometres per minute, what must you multiply by to work out the speed in kilometres per hour?

IN THE COCKPIT

When you're in the cockpit of a jet fighter, you need to be able to read all the dials and information displays.

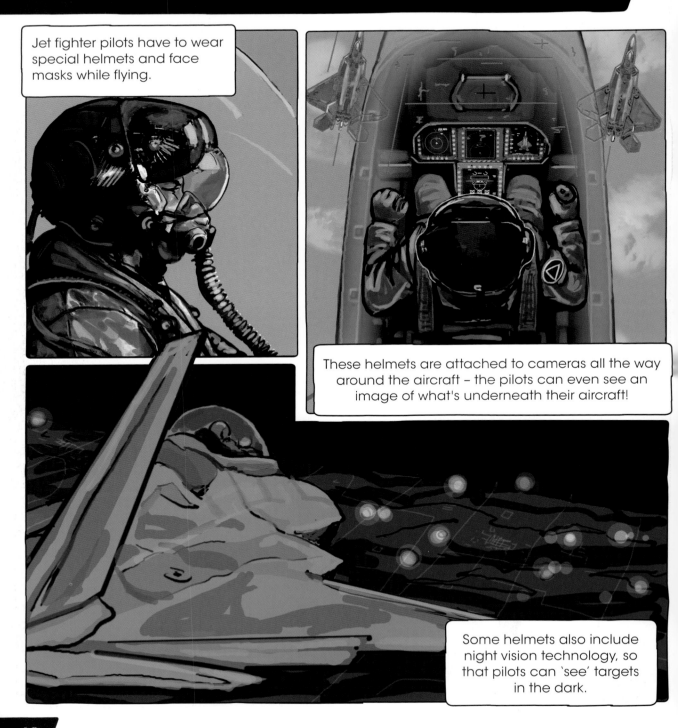

Jet fighter pilots have to wear special helmets and face masks while flying.

These helmets are attached to cameras all the way around the aircraft – the pilots can even see an image of what's underneath their aircraft!

Some helmets also include night vision technology, so that pilots can 'see' targets in the dark.

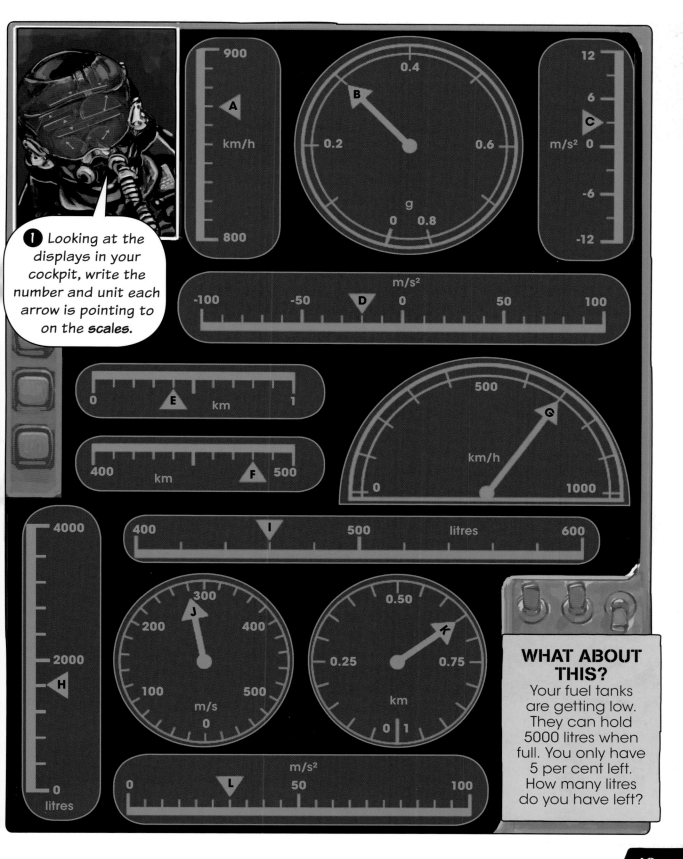

FORMATION FLYING

When flying with the rest of your squadron, you will have to fly close together in formation (organised patterns).

Here are some simple flying formations.

1 Write how many jets are in formation:

a) 1 b) 2 c) 3 d) 4.

2 Name the shapes made by the jets in formation:

a) 1 b) 2 c) 3 d) 4.

3 **Triangular numbers** are special numbers that can be arranged in a triangle. Each row in the triangle has one more than the row in front of it. Triangular numbers include 3, 6 and 10.

This picture shows six jets in a triangular formation. Row 2 has one more jet than row 1, and row 3 has one more jet than row 2.

a) Write out the first six triangular numbers.
b) Is it possible for 36 jets to fly in a triangular formation?

Row 1
Row 2
Row 3

WHAT ABOUT THIS?
Four jets fly in a square formation with the same number in each row and column. How many more jets are needed to make the next largest square formation?

21

G-FORCE

When performing aerobatic twists and turns in your jet fighter, you will experience high g-forces (gravitational forces).

G-forces pull on you and can make you feel heavier. You will have the same experience when riding a roller coaster.

1-g feels the same as the Earth's normal pull of gravity. 2-g makes you feel twice as heavy, 3-g makes you feel three times as heavy and so on. Pilots train to cope with g-forces inside a large machine called a centrifuge.

WOOOSH!

Making very sharp turns in a jet fighter can create g-forces of up to 12-g! High g-forces can damage the human body.

G-suits are worn by pilots to help protect them. These suits allow pilots to withstand more extreme manoeuvres than they would without the suit.

G-suits are really helpful when making sharp turns or spinning upside-down.

Scientists use units called newtons (N) to measure weight.

1 For a pilot weighing 800 N, write how heavy he would feel at:

a) 2-g b) 3-g c) 4-g d) 5-g e) 6-g f) 7-g
g) 8-g h) 9-g i) 10-g j) 11-g k) 12-g.

2 A fighter pilot experiences 3-g during a manoeuvre. How heavy would she feel if she normally weighs:

a) 370 N? b) 430 N? c) 570 N? d) 680 N?

3 This picture shows a jet fighter making a turn. How many degrees has the fighter turned through?

WHAT ABOUT THIS?
It is possible to feel a g-force of zero, or 0-g, when you feel weightless. This can happen when a jet is in a dive. Find your own weight and see what you would weigh at 0-g, 1-g, 2-g, 3-g, 4-g and so on.

WEATHER DATA

A jet fighter pilot needs to understand weather conditions. Clouds can cause turbulence and if the wind is blowing strongly, it could blow you off course.

This **line graph** shows the strength and direction of the wind during one day.

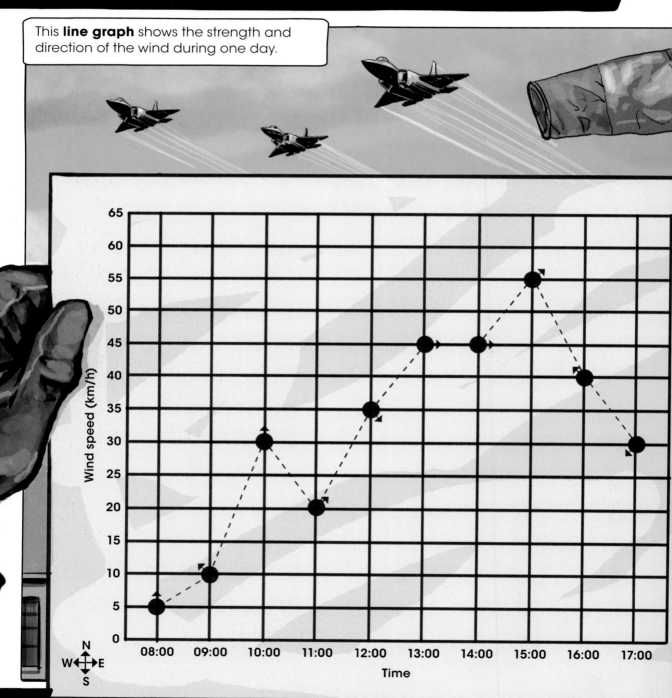

1 What is the speed of the wind at:

a) 09:00? b) 12:00? c) 14:00? d) 16:00? e) 09:30? f) 12:30?

2 At which time or times during the day is the wind:

a) 35 km/h? b) 40 km/h? c) 20 km/h? d) 30 km/h?

3 Write the direction the wind is going at each hour between 08:00 and 17:00.

4 At which time of day is the wind the strongest?

5 Jet fighter pilots must adjust their direction if there is a strong wind. This line shows the direction the pilot will fly to reach the target when the wind is from the north. What is the **angle** between the flight direction and the direction to the target in the picture below?

wind from north

flight direction

direction to the target

WHAT ABOUT THIS?

Look at today's weather forecast. What is the wind speed? What is the wind direction? How might you need to adjust your flying to take these into account?

RECONNAISSANCE

One of your tasks is to fly over enemy positions, taking photographs. This is known as a reconnaissance mission.

A jet fighter has cameras for taking pictures of the location.

A reconnaissance mission gathers information about a particular place. The aim could be to look for possible targets or find out the enemy's position.

This photo was taken on a reconnaissance mission.

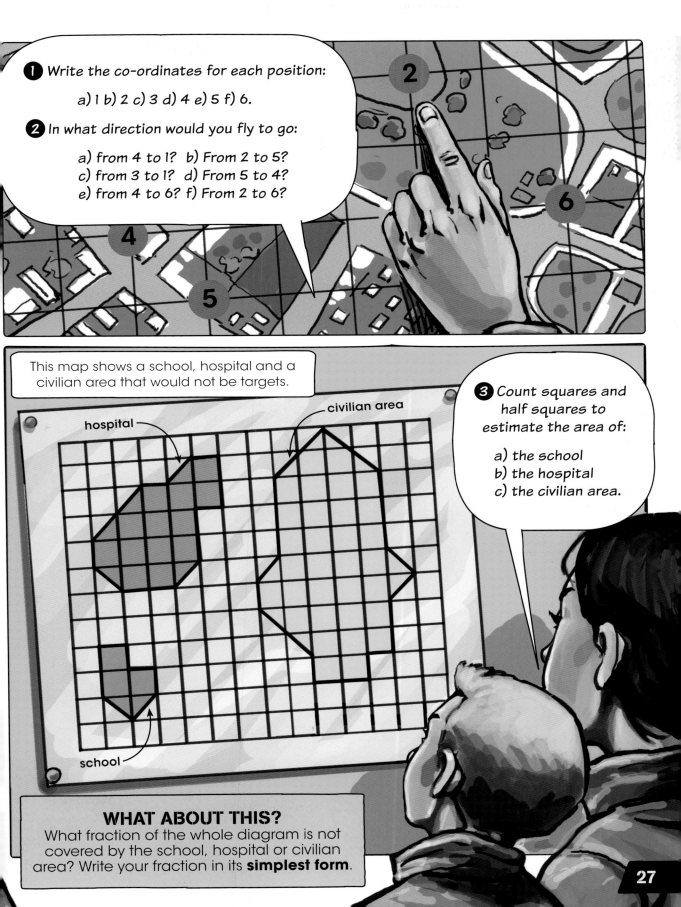

① Write the co-ordinates for each position:

a) 1 b) 2 c) 3 d) 4 e) 5 f) 6.

② In what direction would you fly to go:

a) from 4 to 1? b) From 2 to 5?
c) from 3 to 1? d) From 5 to 4?
e) from 4 to 6? f) From 2 to 6?

This map shows a school, hospital and a civilian area that would not be targets.

hospital

civilian area

school

③ Count squares and half squares to estimate the area of:

a) the school
b) the hospital
c) the civilian area.

WHAT ABOUT THIS?
What fraction of the whole diagram is not covered by the school, hospital or civilian area? Write your fraction in its **simplest form**.

27

AIR-TO-AIR COMBAT

When flying, your jet fighter can be turned in three different ways. These are known as roll, yaw and pitch.

If a jet is flying forwards in a straight line it can be rolled so one wing is lower than the other one.

Yaw means a turn which, when flying **horizontally**, turns the jet to point to a different compass direction.

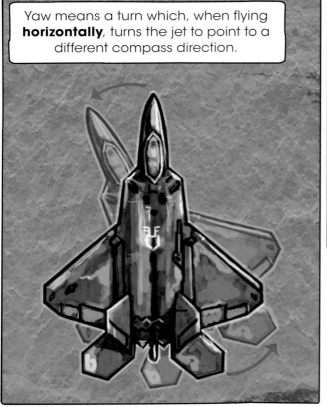

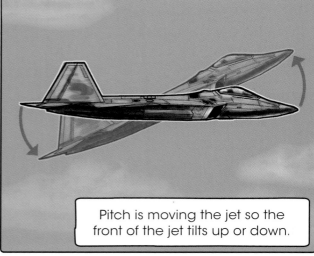

Pitch is moving the jet so the front of the jet tilts up or down.

1 Describe the series of turns shown in these pictures, saying how many right angles or half-right angle turns are being made each time. Include the words 'clockwise' and 'anticlockwise' in your descriptions.

A.

B.

C.

2 Which of these pictures shows jet fighters flying on **parallel** flight-paths?

A.

B.

C.

D.

E.

WHAT ABOUT THIS?
Which of the jets in question 2 are flying horizontally? Which are flying **vertically**?

29

ANSWERS

Congratulations! Your squadron is ready for action! Check your answers here and see how well you did.

PAGES 4–5

1. a) 150 km/h b) 220 km/h c) 370 km/h
   d) 450 km/h e) 530 km/h f) 660 km/h

2. 2400 km/h

3. a) 15 b) 30

4. a) 1320 km/h b) 1440 km/h
   c) 2280 km/h d) 1800 km/h

PAGES 6–7

1. a) Chengdu J-10 b) Chengdu J-10
   c) F-22 Raptor d) Chengdu J-10

2. Eurofighter Typhoon

3. a) 3.41 m, b) 47 cm, c) 3.23 m

4. a) 18,723 kg b) 4223 kg c) 6200 kg

PAGES 8–9

1. The turbojet was invented.

2. MiG 19

3. 16

4. 64

5. F-22 Raptor

6. 67

PAGES 10–11

1. Approximately: a) $\frac{1}{4}$ b) $\frac{1}{3}$ c) $\frac{1}{8}$ d) $\frac{1}{12}$

2. Approximately: a) $\frac{3}{4}$ b) $\frac{2}{3}$ c) $\frac{7}{8}$ d) $\frac{11}{12}$

3. a) 6 months b) 8 months c) 3 months
   d) 2 months e) 5 months

WHAT ABOUT THIS? The jet fighter spent
4 months in air-to-air combat.

PAGES 12–13

1. 5

2. Theo, Emily, Deepa, Simon, Julia, Devon

3. Theo, Emily, Devon (male, female and male)

PAGES 14–15

1. a) seven o'clock
   b) half past nine
   c) quarter to eleven
   d) five to four
   e) twenty to five

2. a) 30 minutes b) 75 minutes c) 45 minutes
   d) 80 minutes

3. a) Physical training
   b) Morning briefing
   c) Studying weather conditions
   d) Simulated flight practice
   e) Flight grading
   f) Daily written exam

WHAT ABOUT THIS? A pilot will spend
576 hours training.

PAGES 16–17

1. 3.9 km

2. 150 kilometres per hour

3. a) 1 hour, b) ½ hour or 30 minutes
   c) ¼ hour or 15 minutes

4. a) 6 km, b) 12 km, c) 18 km, d) 30 km

5. a) 6 minutes b) 9 minutes

6. 4 minutes

WHAT ABOUT THIS? You would need to
multiply it by 60. 12 x 60 = 720 km/h.

PAGES 18–19

1. a) 870 km/h b) 0.3-g c) 3 m/s^2
   d) -20 m/s^2 e) 0.4 km f) 480 km
   g) 700 km/h h) 1800 litres i) 460 litres
   j) 280 m/s k) 0.65 km l) 30 m/s^2

WHAT ABOUT THIS? The tanks have 250
litres of fuel left.

PAGES 20–21

1. a) 9 b) 4 c) 5 d) 5

2. a) square b) rhombus c) pentagon
   d) trapezium

3. a) 1, 3, 6, 10, 15, 21 b) yes

WHAT ABOUT THIS? Five more jets are
needed to make the next largest square
formation (nine in total).

PAGES 22–23

1. a) 1600 N b) 2400 N
   c) 3200 N d) 4000 N
   e) 4800 N f) 5600 N
   g) 6400 N h) 7200 N
   i) 8000 N j) 8800 N
   k) 9600 N

2. a) 1110 N b) 1290 N
   c) 1710 N d) 2040 N

3. 180°

PAGES 24–25

1. a) 10 km/h b) 35 km/h c) 45 km/h
   d) 40 km/h e) 20 km/h f) 40 km/h

2. a) 12:00 and 16:30 b) 12:30 and 16:00 c) 9:30
   and 11:00 d) 10:00, 11:30 and 17:00

3. 08:00 North, 09:00 North West, 10:00 North,
   11:00 North East, 12:00 South East, 13:00
   East, 14:00 East, 15:00 North East, 16:00
   North West, 17:00 South West

4. 15:00

5. 15°

PAGES 26–27

1. a) (2, 6) b) (6, 5) c) (9, 6) d) (2, 3)
   e) (3, 2) f) (8, 3)

2. a) North b) South West c) West
   d) North West e) East f) South East

3. a) 4 squares b) 15½ squares c) 36½ squares

WHAT ABOUT THIS? 112/168 or ⅔

PAGES 28–29

1. a) right angle turn clockwise, half right angle
   turn clockwise, half right angle turn
   clockwise, two right angled turn (clockwise
   or anticlockwise)
   b) half right angle turn anticlockwise, half
   right angle turn anticlockwise, two right
   angled turns (clockwise or anticlockwise),
   right angle turn clockwise
   c) right angle anticlockwise, half right angle
   turn clockwise, right angle turn
   anticlockwise, half right angle turn clockwise.

2. a, b and e pairs are parallel

WHAT ABOUT THIS? The jets in 'A' are
horizontal and the jets in 'B' are vertical.

GLOSSARY

ANGLE
An angle is an amount of turn. It is measured in degrees, such as 90°, which is also known as a right angle.

AREA
The area of a shape is the amount of surface it covers.

ASCEND
Ascend means going up.

DESCEND
Descend means going down.

FRACTION
A part of a whole. The number on the bottom (the denominator) tells you how many parts the whole has been split into. The number on the top (the numerator) tells you the number of equal parts being described.

HORIZONTALLY
When something is going from side to side, like the horizon.

LINE GRAPH
A line graph shows information by using points and lines on a grid.

PARALLEL
Parallel lines stay the same distance apart along their entire length. No matter how long the lines are, they would never meet.

SCALES
Scales are usually divided into equal sections and have a marker, such as an arrow, to show values. It is important to work out the value of each section to find the marked value.

SIMPLEST FORM
A fraction can be written in its simplest form by dividing the numerator (top number) and denominator (bottom number) by the largest number possible.

TIMELINE
A timeline is a line that shows events in chronological (date) order.

TRIANGULAR NUMBERS
A triangular number can be drawn as a pattern of dots to make a triangle. Examples include 1, 3, 6 and 10. The sequence follows a +2, +3, +4, +5... pattern.

VERTICALLY
When something goes straight up.

INDEX